The Collector's Series / Volume 14

SUPER SOUPS

by Sally Meddock

The
AMERICAN
★ COOKING ★
GUILD™

Boynton Beach, Florida

Acknowledgments
—Cover Design and Layout by Pearl & Associates, Inc.
—Cover Photo by Burwell and Burwell

More...Quick Recipes for Creative Cooking!
The American Cooking Guild's *Collector's Series* includes over 30 popular cooking topics such as Barbeque, Breakfast & Brunches, Chicken, Cookies, Hors d' Oeuvres, Seafood, Tea, Coffee, Pasta, Pizza, Salads, Italian and many more. Each book contains more than 50 selected recipes. For a catalog of these and many other full sized cookbooks, send $1 to the address below and a coupon will be included for $1 off your first order.

Cookbooks Make Great Premiums!
The American Cooking Guild has been the premier publisher of private label and custom cookbooks since 1981. Retailers, manufacturers, and food companies have all chosen The American Cooking Guild to publish their premium and promotional cookbooks. For further information on our special market programs, please contact the address below.

The American Cooking Guild
3600-K South Congress Avenue
Boynton Beach, FL 33426

Contents

Introduction

I derive great pleasure from soups. Creating them, sharing recipes with friends, and tasting them. Soups are easy to prepare and they're so versatile. Soup can be served as an appetizer, as a first course or as a meal in itself. There are even soup recipes for wonderfully different desserts.

The real beauty of soups is that they can be created from almost any combination of ingredients. The only limit is your imagination. Soup cookery is easy, and in no time you'll be experimenting with confidence.

Some soups can be made in a matter of minutes while others are best after an all-day cooking session. Nothing can beat the mouth-watering aromas that will fill your house from that one pot of soup simmering on the stove.

Soup can make a difference in the way that you feel. Everyone knows how good chicken soup is when you have a cold, but no one seems to know why. And what about, the refreshing taste of an icy gazpacho on a hot summer day, or a hearty vegetable soup on a blustery winter evening? Somehow, soup always seems to satisfy.

In the interest of good health, I have omitted salt from these recipes. You may want to add salt to your taste, but I believe that I have compensated for the lack of salt with the addition of herbs and various savory ingredients. This is not to say that these recipes are sodium-free, but rather low-sodium. There are already many products that you use in these recipes that contain "hidden" salts (i.e. commercial stocks, butter, cheese, etc.); therefore the addition of salt is unnecessary. If you are embarking on a low-sodium diet, please test-taste your soup first before adjusting the seasoning. You may find that you'll be pleasantly surprised by the intensity of the unsalted flavors.

Even though there are specific measurements in these recipes, to the creative cook any soup is a candidate for "experimental" adjustments.

Now, on to the healthy and delicious world of soups!

Things You Should Know About Soup Ingredients

This section will help you to make creative substitutions and additions by giving you a better understanding of the nature of common soup ingredients.

Cream: Because of the high fat content of heavy cream, you may substitute light cream, half 'n' half, regular, low-fat or non-fat milk in any recipe calling for cream. However, the thickness of the soup will decrease along with the lower fat content of the liquid you choose to add. This can be remedied by increasing the amount of vegetables to be puréed. A bit more flour may be added as well, to develop the consistency of the soup as originally intended in the recipe. Use no substitutes when making whipped cream for garnishes; only whipping or heavy cream will suffice.

Sour Cream: Plain low-fat yogurt can always be substituted for sour cream. It has similar flavor, similar consistency, and it is lower in fat and calories.

Cheese: Cheese is one of the ingredients full of "hidden" salts. There are several brands of low-sodium cheeses available in the markets today that may be substituted for regular cheese. However, the lack of salt may be noticeable in your soup and may require an increase in the other seasonings.

Butter: Regular butter contains salt as well as a high fat content. You can use unsalted butter instead. Margarine, or diet margarine, is difficult to use because of its high water content. You may have to use twice as much to compensate for water evaporation.

Olive Oil: The term "extra virgin" olive oil means that the oil is from the first and most flavorful pressing of olives. "Virgin" is from the next pressing and is better suited for use in soups because it is not overpowering or too redolent of olives. Any vegetable oil may be used if olive oil is not specified.

Cooking Sherries and Wines: I learned a long time ago that if a wine isn't good enough to drink, then it isn't good enough to cook with! The term "cooking wine" or "cooking sherry" is simply telling you that the contents of the bottle are not fit to be table wine. Now why would any chef want a "cooking wine" in his or her best dish? Always follow the recommendations of "dry" or "sweet" for the wine or sherry being used.

Herbs and Spices: Always use fresh or fresh-dried herbs and spices whenever possible for the finest flavor in your recipes. Dried packaged products may be used whenever fresh are not available. If you are using fresh herbs and spices, be aware that you'll need almost twice as much as called for in these recipes since they are geared towards using dried products. For some of the more exotic spices, any specialty, gourmet or import store usually carries them or will order them for you.

When shopping for parsley, any type available may be used without worrying about a flavor change.

To alleviate any confusion, cilantro and coriander are one and the same plant. Cilantro is simply the name by which it is sold in Latino and Southern United States markets. It is known as coriander everywhere else in the world. Cilantro/coriander is available fresh or dried.

If you see names of herbs or spices that you do not recognize, consult a cooking dictionary or an herb book. Herb books are very helpful in suggesting substitutions when the particular plant you want isn't available or in season. Don't be afraid to start your own herb garden. Or, you may want to consider an indoor window pot for your favorite herb.

Freezing Soups

If you plan on freezing soups and stocks, keep a couple of cases of jars made specifically for freezing on hand. The jars come in one-pint to one-quart sizes, so you can freeze one portion or more at a time depending on your needs. Remember to leave at least two inches of "breathing" room at the top of the jar so that the glass won't crack with the expansion of the frozen soup. If a jar does crack, throw it away, as it is impossible to account for every sliver of glass when thawing.

There are a few other ways to freeze stocks and consommés besides using jars. The easiest way is to pour the stock into ice cube trays. When frozen, simply pop out the cubes and store them in plastic bags in the freezer. They can be stored this way for up to three months. Another method is to use any freezer-safe metal or plastic container, pour in the particular amount (i.e. one cup), remove when frozen and store in plastic bags. These methods allow for more storage space in your freezer.

Most soups will freeze well with the exception of soups made with eggs. The eggs tend to cook and congeal during the reheating process. Cream soups are made with eggs, but can be frozen as long as they are watched carefully when reheated. If any separation does occur, whirl in the blender to restore the soup to its former consistency.

A good idea for singles or people on the go is to buy a couple of cases of jars for freezing, make a large pot of your favorite soup and freeze it. Hearty, homemade soup is always available in just the time it takes to thaw a jar in the microwave or in a pan of gently boiling water. Be sure to always label and date the jars. Most soups have a freezer life of up to three months but each soup does vary.

Stocks

A good stock is the basic ingredient in most soups so it is worth the time involved to make your stock the very best. Canned stocks may be substituted in any recipe and I am certainly not above using them when pressed for time, or just too lazy to make fresh stock.

A word of caution though—canned stocks are usually strongly flavored and quite high in salt content. In fact, they should be diluted with water whenever they are used.

Once you have developed and mastered the relatively easy art of making a good stock, you will find that there are many uses for stock other than in soup (gravies, sauces and poaching). You'll also find that stocks do not necessarily have to be a time consuming affair, if you do a little advance planning. All stocks freeze well and this enables a cook to make large quantities in one cooking session.

Stock is composed of any meaty bones, vegetables and spices simmered in water for a specified amount of time. The liquid is strained and the resulting stock can be used as a base for your soups or served alone as it is strongly flavored.

There are two categories into which stocks can be divided. Poultry or clear stocks include chicken, turkey, goose and duck. Fish stock or fumet is also included in this group.

Then there is the second category of meat or brown stocks using beef, veal, pork or lamb bones. The main difference between the poultry/white stocks and brown stocks is that with brown stocks the bones are first browned or roasted to bring out a more intense flavor.

Soup bones that are labeled as such did get their names for a reason. Don't be afraid to experiment with any carcass or bones that you have left over. You may come up with some interesting combinations that create a unique taste in your soups.

All of the spices, bay leaves and parsley in a particular recipe may be tied together in a small piece of cheesecloth to form a bouquet garnish. They may be purchased pre-made in gourmet shops as well.

Chicken Stock

A good rule of thumb is to use one pound of poultry parts (necks, backs, wings, etc.) per one quart of water. Giblets may also be used, except for the liver because of its distinct flavor. The water should be cold when poured over the vegetables and bones.

3   pounds chicken parts
3   quarts cold water
1   large onion, quartered
2   ribs celery, including tops, chopped
2   large carrots, pared and roughly chopped
2   leeks, well-rinsed and sliced
1   bay leaf
1   sprig parsley
1   teaspoon each white pepper, sage, basil and marjoram

Combine all ingredients in a large stock pot. Cover, heat to boiling, reduce heat after 1 minute and simmer 3 hours. Skim foam occasionally. It may be necessary to add water to keep all ingredients covered.

Using a double thickness of dampened cheesecloth to line a sieve, strain the stock. To increase the richness of the stock, return to the pot and continue to boil 15 to 30 minutes, uncovered. Depending on the richness, it **makes 1 quart or more of stock.**

To make clear stock, allow to settle after straining. Pour off clear portion very slowly or restrain stock through a fresh cheesecloth. If the stock is not being used immediately, refrigerate for several hours, then degrease by scraping the hardened fat from the surface of the stock.

For turkey, duck, goose and pheasant stocks, put the entire carcass in a pot large enough to hold it comfortably. Be sure to keep the carcass covered with water at all times during cooking. After straining, remove bits of meat from the carcass and reserve for use in other soup recipes (e.g. Turkey or Goose Chowders).

Poultry stocks can be refrigerated 2 to 4 days or frozen up to 2 months.

Fish Stock

Fish stock is the basis for all seafood soups and chowders. There are two main categories of fish—oily and non-oily—to be considered.

The non-oily types are recommended for use in stocks. Non-oily fish include bass, snapper, whiting, cod, flounder, halibut, sole and perch. Local varieties of non-oily fish will be less expensive and most likely to be the freshest available-check with your local fish dealer.

The rule of one pound of fish scraps to one quart of cold water applies.

2 *pounds non-oily fish heads and frames*
2 *quarts cold water*
1 *medium onion, quartered*
2 *ribs celery, including tops, chopped*
2 *cloves garlic, crushed with the flat side of a knife*
2 *sprigs parsley*
2 *Tablespoons lemon juice*
1 *teaspoon each thyme and basil white pepper*

Tie up all fish heads and frames in a cheesecloth. Place in a medium stock pot. Add vegetables and spices. Pour cold water over all ingredients. Cover, bring to a boil, reduce heat and simmer 45 minutes. Skim foam occasionally.

Move the pot to the sink. Tie the cheesecloth to the water faucet and allow to drip back into the pot. When the bag is cool, squeeze very carefully (fish bones are sharp!) for the remaining liquid. Discard bag. Strain stock through a double thickness of dampened cheesecloth lining a sieve. Return stock to the pot and simmer 15 to 30 minutes until desired richness is obtained. An extremely rich version of fish stock is know as fumet.

If a clear stock is desired, allow strained stock to settle. Pour off clear portion very slowly or simply restrain stock through a fresh cheesecloth. Depending on the richness of the stock, it **makes 1 to 2 quarts.**

Fish stock can be refrigerated for 2 days or frozen up to 2 months.

Beef Stock

This hearty combination of beef bones and vegetables is also known as brown stock. Have your butcher crack the bones for you.

6   *pounds lean beef bones, cracked into 2-inch pieces*
1   *large white onion, quartered*
2   *large carrots, pared and chopped*
2-6 *Tablespoons cooking oil*
1   *small rib celery, including top, chopped*
1   *leek, well-rinsed and sliced*
6   *cloves garlic, crushed with the flat side of a knife*
1   *bay leaf*
8   *whole cloves*
8   *whole black peppercorns*
$^1/_2$ *cup tomato juice or 2 whole tomatoes, diced*
1   *teaspoon thyme*
2   *sprigs parsley*
1   *teaspoon lemon juice (or white vinegar)*
4   *quarts cold water*

Place bones, onions and carrots in a large roasting pan. Sprinkle with a little cooking oil and roast at 450° for 45 minutes, tossing occasionally. Transfer roasted bones and vegetables to a large stock pot and add remaining ingredients.

Use a little hot water, red wine or Cognac to deglaze the roasting pan; that is, use liquid to remove the browned bits of meat cooked onto the bottom of the pan. Add deglazing liquid to the stock pot. Cover, bring to a boil, reduce heat and simmer 4 hours or longer. Skim foam occasionally.

Strain stock through a double thickness of dampened cheesecloth lining a sieve. The solids may be reserved for future use in stocks by refrigerating or freezing. This stock can be reduced to form a richer stock, gravy or meat glaze by continuing to simmer after straining.

Variation: Substitute veal or lamb bones for the beef bones in the same amounts.

Makes about 2 quarts depending on the amount of reduction.

Consommés

Made with a base of beef stock, these soups are light and perfect for luncheon first courses. Be sure not to freeze any consommés that contain eggs. All others will keep frozen up to 2 months.

Beef Consommé

A richer, more elegant version of beef stock

> 1 *carrot*
> 1 *medium onion*
> 1 *rib celery*
> 4 *cups extra-rich (or reduced) beef stock*
> 1/2 *pound lean ground beef sour cream or plain yogurt parsley sprigs*

Mince carrot, onion and celery in a food processor or by hand. Combine all ingredients in a large saucepan. Cover, bring to a boil, reduce heat and simmer 1 hour. Strain consommé through a cheese-cloth-lined sieve. Discard solids.

Serve hot and garnish with a dollop of sour cream or plain yogurt and a sprig of parsley. Melba toast is just the right accompaniment to this light meal.

Makes 4 servings.

Jellied Beef Consommé

(Prepare 1 Day Ahead)

A slightly more time-consuming way to dress up your beef consommé. It's also a nice change of pace if you're eating soups for slimming purposes.

Follow the preceding recipe for Beef Consommé. Chill 1 cup of consommé for 2 hours to determine firmness. If already firm, no gelatin is needed. If semi-firm, use 1 envelope of gelatin. If still liquid, use 2 envelopes.

Return chilled portion of consommé to original batch and add appropriate amount of gelatin. Heat and stir until gelatin is dissolved. Chill until firm. Break up with a fork.

Serve in chilled glass bowls for best effect. Garnish with a wedge of lemon and a sprig of parsley.

Makes 4 servings.

Consommé Madrilène

A traditional consommé served either hot or jellied.

> 1   *can (16 ounces) tomatoes, undrained*
> 3   *cups beef stock*
> $^1/_2$ *pound lean ground beef*
> 1   *leek, white part only, finely chopped*
> 1   *carrot, shredded*
> 1   *egg white*
>   *dash of cayenne pepper*
> 1   *Tablespoon fresh parsley, minced*
> $^1/_4$ *cup dry sherry*
>   *ground black pepper, to taste sour cream*
>   *red or black caviar*

Purée tomatoes and their juice. In a large saucepan combine stock, tomato purée, beef, leek, carrot, egg white, cayenne and parsley. Bring to a boil, reduce heat to low and simmer, partially covered, 1 hour. Do not stir.

Strain soup through a double thickness of dampened cheesecloth. Allow consommé to drip through the sieve very slowly for greater clarity. Discard solids and return consommé to the saucepan. Heat thoroughly, skimming foam.

Add sherry and pepper to taste. Serve hot and garnish with a dollop of sour cream and a dot of red or black caviar.

Makes 4 servings.

Jellied Consommé Madrilène

(Prepare 1 Day Ahead)

Follow the recipe for Consommé Madrilène. Refrigerate soup overnight. Scrape off solid fat that forms on the surface. If consommé has not jelled, use ratio of gelatin to consommé as described in the Jellied Beef Consommé recipe. When consommé has jelled, break up with a fork.

Serve in chilled glass bowls. Garnish with traditional toppings of sour cream and red or black caviar.

Makes 4 servings.

Variations For Consommé

Consommé Champignon: Sauté ½ pound fresh white mushrooms in 2 tablespoons of butter for 5 minutes. Add mushrooms to 4 cups of beef stock and heat thoroughly. Add 1 tablespoon dry sherry and 1/4 teaspoon tarragon. Purée in a blender or food processor. Return to stove and reheat. Serve hot and garnish with a sprig of parsley and float a few mushroom slices on top.

Makes 4 servings.

Vegetable Consommé: Cut 1 carrot, 1 leek and 1 zucchini into matchstick pieces. Add ¼ cup shredded lettuce or spinach, ¼ cup sliced mushrooms. Carefully sauté in 2 tablespoons butter for 8 minutes. Add 4 cups beef stock and heat thoroughly. Be careful not to break vegetable pieces during cooking.

Makes 4 servings.

Vegetable

Garlic Vegetable Soup

The garlic adds a touch of gourmet taste to otherwise plain vegetables. This soup is satisfying enough to be served as a main course for dinner.

2 cups tomatoes, peeled and diced
2 cups garbanzo beans, drained
2 large onions, chopped
2 ribs celery, chopped
3 medium zucchini (Italian squash), diced
6-8 cloves garlic, minced
2 cups dry white wine
3 Tablespoons fresh parsley, minced
1 bay leaf
1 teaspoon each paprika and black pepper
$^{1}/_{2}$ teaspoon basil
$^{1}/_{4}$ teaspoon thyme
2 cups cream
$1^{1}/_{2}$ cups Monterey Jack cheese, grated
$^{1}/_{2}$ cup Romano cheese, grated

Combine all of the ingredients, except the cream and cheeses, in a medium-sized oven-proof casserole with handles. Cover and simmer on the range 1 hour over medium heat or until vegetables are tender. Remove from heat. Discard bay leaf. Stir in cream and cheeses. Bake, uncovered, at 325° 10 minutes.

Serve with Italian style bread and garlic butter.

Makes 6 to 8 servings.

Lighten Up: To lower fat and calories, substitute the following for the heavy cream. In a saucepan, combine 1/2 cup nonfat dry milk, 3 tablespoons cornstarch and 2 cups water. Stir over low heat until thick, then add to soup in place of cream.

Pumpkin Soup

Here is a pumpkin soup recipe with an interesting variation, perfect for serving during the fall and winter holiday seasons. You can use fresh or canned pumpkin purée (or any winter squash-Hubbard, acorn or butternut). This, and the following recipe, are to be enjoyed as first courses.

1   yellow onion, finely chopped
2   Tablespoons butter
2   Tablespoons flour
2   pounds pumpkin purée*, fresh or canned
5   cups chicken stock
$^{1}/_{4}$ cup white vermouth or dry sherry (optional)
$^{1}/_{2}$ teaspoon ginger
$^{1}/_{4}$ teaspoon nutmeg
2   egg yolks
1   cup heavy cream pinch of mace

*To cook fresh pumpkin or any winter squash, rinse shell well and slice crosswise to form halves. Scoop out seeds and strings. Place flesh side down on a heavy-duty baking sheet. Cook in a medium oven (350°) 1 hour or until pumpkin is fork tender. Scoop out flesh and purée in a food processor, blender or food mill. It is now ready for addition to your recipe.

In a medium soup pot, sauté onion in butter 3 minutes. Stir in flour. Add pumpkin purée and stock. Add optional vermouth or sherry at this time. Cover and simmer 15 minutes, then add spices.

Combine egg yolks and cream. Spoon a little of the hot soup into the egg-cream mixture. Return to the soup and blend. Heat soup until hot but **do not allow to boil.**

Makes 6 servings.

Pumpkin-Apple Soup: Follow the Pumpkin Soup recipe above, adding 2 medium tart apples (Granny Smith or Pippins), peeled, cored and sliced with the pumpkin purée. Simmer until the apples are soft, about 30 minutes. Add 2 tablespoons bourbon, whiskey or brandy (optional).

Makes 6 servings.

Tuscany Bean Soup

1   pound dried Great Northern beans, rinsed,
     drained and picked over
2   cups chicken stock
1   bay leaf
1   teaspoon marjoram
2   Tablespoons olive oil
2   medium white onions, chopped
2   cloves garlic, minced
$1^1/_2$ cups carrots, sliced
2   large potatoes, pared and cubed
1   package frozen chopped spinach, or,
1   large bunch fresh spinach, well-rinsed and chopped

In a large soup pot, combine beans and 3 quarts of water. Discard any beans that float to the surface. Cover and boil 3 minutes over high heat. Remove from heat and allow to stand 1 hour.

Add chicken stock, bay leaf and marjoram. Bring to a boil, reduce heat and simmer, covered, 1 hour.

Heat oil in a large skillet and sauté onions, carrots and garlic 5 minutes. Add sauté mixture and remaining ingredients to the pot. Cover and continue to simmer until potatoes are tender, about 45 minutes. Remove bay leaf before serving.

Makes 6 to 8 servings.

Vegetable-Cheese Soup

The addition of cheese is a real kid pleaser. Do not cook the vegetables overlong if you want your soup to look bright and colorful.

*1   large potato, pared and diced
*1   large carrot, pared and diced
*1   rib celery, chopped
 1   cup water
 1   medium white onion, chopped
 4   Tablespoons butter
 2   Tablespoons flour
 2   cups chicken stock
1¹/₂ cups cream
 2   cups sharp cheddar cheese, grated
     minced fresh parsley
     paprika

*Any firm-textured vegetable such as cauliflower, broccoli, turnips, etc. may be substituted in approximately the same amount.

Place the first 3 vegetables and water in a small covered saucepan and heat to boiling. Reduce heat to medium and continue cooking 10 to 12 minutes. Set vegetables and their liquid aside.

In a medium soup pot, sauté onion in butter 5 minutes. Stir in flour. Gradually whisk in stock and cream. Stirring continuously, cook until thickened, but not boiling, over low heat. Stir in cheese until melted. Add reserved vegetables and their liquid.

Season with parsley and paprika. Reheat soup until hot. Best when served within the the hour.

Makes 6 servings.

Lighten Up: To lower fat and calories, substitute the following for the heavy cream. In a saucepan, combine 1/4 cup nonfat dry milk, 2 tablespoons cornstarch and 1¹/₂ cups water. Stir over low heat until thick, then add to soup in place of cream.

Leek Soup

This is comforting and warming on a cold night: thick and hearty, tinged with smoky bacon and topped with Brie. Serve with a crisp French bread and a green salad with lots of crunch.

6   slices bacon, in 1" pieces
1   leek, sliced
1   medium onion, sliced
1   Tablespoon vegetable oil
1   medium boiling potato, peeled and sliced
2   cups grated cabbage
4   cups chicken broth
1   teaspoon dried oregano
3   ounces Brie cheese, rind removed, cut into $1/2$" cubes
    salt and pepper to taste
    chopped parsley as a garnish

In a large, heavy saucepan fry the bacon, leek and onion in the oil until softened. Don't let the onion brown. Add potato and cook until the bacon begins to brown. Add the cabbage and mix well. Add chicken broth, oregano, and salt and pepper to taste. Cover and simmer for 20 minutes.

Cool slightly. Place the soup in the blender or food processor and purée. Return it to the pan and heat to boiling.

To serve, divide the cheese among 4 soup bowls and pour the hot soup over. Sprinkle with parsley.

Makes 4 servings.

Spinach Soup

3 Tablespoons butter
3 Tablespoons flour
6 cups chicken stock
$^1/_2$ cup dry white wine
2 carrots, pared and diced
2 medium zucchini (Italian squash), diced
$^1/_4$ cup fresh parsley, minced
1 pound broad-leaf spinach, well-rinsed and stemmed
1 cup heavy cream
  white pepper
  finely chopped white onion, for garnish

In a large saucepan, melt butter over low heat. Add flour, blend well and continue cooking 2 minutes. Whisk in stock and wine. Add carrots, zucchini and parsley. Cover and simmer until carrots are soft, about 20 minutes.

Meanwhile, lightly and quickly process spinach in a food processor, blender or finely chop by hand. Set spinach aside to be added later. Strain stock/vegetable soup mixture through a fine sieve. Return stock to the saucepan, purée vegetables, then re-add them to stock in sauce pan. Add the reserved spinach. Stir in cream and heat until very hot but not boiling. Season to taste with white pepper. Garnish with finely chopped white onion.

This can be frozen for up to 1 month.

Makes 6 to 8 servings.

Tomato and Green Chile Soup

This is a thick soup with lots of things in it. The Polish sausage and green chilies give it a rich, spicy flavor. Use mild or hot chilies.

1   can (16 ounces) diced tomatoes
6   ounces Polish sausage, sliced thin
1   cup onions, sliced thin
1   cup carrots, quartered lengthwise, then sliced thin
1   can (4 ounces) diced green chilies
4   ounces small mushrooms, halved
1   cup chicken broth
    salt and pepper to taste

Put tomatoes into a large saucepan along with the sausage, onions, carrots, green chilies, mushrooms and broth.

Bring the mixture to a boil over high heat. Cover, lower the heat and simmer for 25 minutes. Add salt and pepper to taste.

Makes 4 servings.

20-Minute Vegetable Beef Soup

Here is a gem: a vegetable soup you can make in 20 minutes. The secret is to use canned vegetables. This recipe makes a big pot of soup, enough for dinner and a couple of containers for the freezer.

1   pound ground beef
1   Tablespoon olive oil
1   large onion, chopped
1/4   medium head of cabbage, shredded
1   can (15 ounces) carrots with their liquid
1   can (14 to 16 ounces) tomatoes
1   can (15 ounces) kidney beans, drained and rinsed
1   can (15 ounces) cannellini beans, drained and rinsed
1   can (15 ounces) corn, drained
6   cups low-sodium chicken broth
1   can green beans, drained
3/4   cup small elbow macaroni
1/2   teaspoon salt, or to taste
1/2   teaspoon dried oregano
1/2   teaspoon dried thyme
1/4   teaspoon pepper
    grated Parmesan cheese for garnish

In a large pot, sauté the ground beef in the olive oil until it is no longer pink.

Add the onion and cabbage to the meat and stir and cook over medium-high heat until the vegetables start to wilt, about 5 minutes. Add the remaining ingredients.

Bring the soup to a boil, lower the heat and simmer for 20 to 45 minutes.

Swirl 1 tablespoon Parmesan cheese into each serving.

Makes 12 servings.

Tortilla Soup

Hearty and good. Pass a bowl of crushed corn chips along with the Cheddar and sour cream. This is delicious on a chilly winter evening.

$1/2$ pound lean ground beef
$1/4$ cup chopped onions
$1^3/4$ cups water
  1   can (16 ounces) chopped stewed tomatoes, undrained
  1   can (16 ounces) pinto beans, drained and rinsed
  1   can (8 ounces) tomato sauce
  2   Tablespoons taco seasoning mix (half a package)
      crushed corn chips as a garnish
      shredded Cheddar cheese as a garnish
      sour cream as a garnish

In a large saucepan cook the beef and onion over medium heat until the meat is browned. Add water, tomatoes and their liquid, beans, tomato sauce and seasoning mix.

Cover and simmer over medium-low heat for 20 to 30 minutes.

Pass bowls of crushed corn chips, cheese and sour cream to top each serving.

Makes 4 to 6 servings.

Bisques and Cream Soups

Bisques are cream soups traditionally based on seafood ingredients but easily adapted to your favorite vegetables. These recipes are equally good when served chilled.

Tomato Bisque

1¹/₂ *Tablespoons butter*
2 *medium onions, chopped*
2 *cloves garlic, minced*
2 *cups chicken stock*
1 *can (28 ounces) whole tomatoes, undrained*
¹/₄ *cup brown rice, uncooked*
1 *pinch each, basil and thyme*
2 *cups light cream*
   dash of cayenne pepper

In a large saucepan, sauté onions and garlic in butter until soft but not brown. Add stock, tomatoes, rice, basil and thyme. Cover, bring to a boil, reduce heat and simmer 45 minutes.

Purée all of soup in a food processor or blender. Strain soup through a cheesecloth-lined sieve and discard solids. Return soup to the pot and add cream. Blend and heat soup through. Garnish with a sprinkle of chopped parsley.

Makes 4 servings.

Lighten Up: To lower fat and calories, substitute the following for the heavy cream. In a saucepan, combine 1/2 cup nonfat dry milk, 3 tablespoons cornstarch and 2 cups water. Stir over low heat until thick, then add to soup in place of cream.

Zucchini-Onion Bisque

Be sure to leave zucchini unpeeled for the light green coloring it adds to the soup.

  4 *cups chicken stock*
  2 *medium White Rose potatoes, pared and chopped*
  2 *large onions, chopped*
  3 *medium zucchini (Italian squash), sliced*
  3 *cloves garlic, minced*
1¹/₂ *cups heavy cream*
     white or cayenne pepper

In a large covered saucepan, combine stock, potatoes, onions, zucchini and garlic. Cover, bring to a boil, reduce heat, and simmer 30 minutes. Strain soup through a sieve.

Purée solids in a food processor or blender. Stir purée back into the stock and return soup to saucepan. Slowly whisk in cream. Season to taste with white or cayenne pepper depending on the spiciness you prefer.

Makes 6 servings.

Ham and Corn Bisque

A wonderful soup studded with little nuggets of smoky ham and sweet corn kernels. Serve it with cornbread.

2 cups diced cooked ham
1 cup chopped celery
$^{1}/_{2}$ cup chopped onion
$^{1}/_{4}$ cup butter
2 cans (16 ounces each) cream-style corn
1 cup milk
$^{1}/_{2}$ teaspoon celery salt
$^{1}/_{2}$ teaspoon garlic powder
$^{1}/_{2}$ teaspoon pepper

In a large saucepan sauté the ham, celery and onion in butter until tender. Add the corn, milk, celery salt, garlic powder and pepper.

Bring to a boil. Reduce the heat, cover and simmer for 20 minutes. Serve hot.

Makes 6 servings.

Basic Cream Soup

For a full-bodied soup, reserve a few pieces of the main vegetable to be added during the last 10 minutes of cooking. I suggest steaming them first as they will be quite crunchy otherwise.

    1   medium onion, chopped
    3   Tablespoons butter
    3   Tablespoons flour
    4   cups chicken stock
  2–3   cups any firm-textured vegetable, rinsed and chopped
         (broccoli, asparagus, parsley, etc,)
    2   egg yolks
  $^{1}/_{2}$ cup light cream
         reserved pieces of vegetable
         white pepper

Sauté onion in butter over medium heat in a large saucepan until onion is soft but not brown. Stir in flour. Whisk in stock and add vegetable. Cover and simmer 15 minutes. Separate liquids from solids through strainer. Purée solids in a food processor or blender.

Return liquid and purée to the saucepan. Beat egg yolks and cream together. Spoon a little of the hot soup into the egg-cream mixture and stir. Return mixture to the soup. Toss in reserved vegetable pieces and cook over low heat 10 minutes. Add white pepper to taste.

Makes 4 servings.

Cream Of Mushroom Soup

$3/4$ pounds fresh white mushrooms, finely chopped
2   Tablespoons butter
1 $1/2$ Tablespoons cornstarch
2   cups chicken stock
1 $1/2$ cups light cream
1   teaspoon Worcestershire sauce

Sauté mushrooms in butter in a medium soup pot for 10 minutes. Stir in cornstarch and whisk in stock. Stirring continuously, cook 5 minutes. Lower the heat and simmer, covered, 15 minutes.

Purée half of the soup in a food processor or blender and return to the pot. Add the cream and Worcestershire sauce. Stir and heat until very hot.

Makes 4 servings.

Cream of Walnut

2   Tablespoons butter
2   Tablespoons flour
1   small onion, chopped
2   cups chicken stock
$1^1/2$ cups English walnuts*, finely chopped
    dash each white pepper, celery powder and nutmeg
$1^1/2$ cups light cream

*Pecans, cashews, peanuts or macadamias may be substituted.

In a medium saucepan, sauté onion in butter 5 minutes. Stir in flour and cook 1 minute. Slowly whisk in stock. Cook over medium heat until slightly thickened, about 8 minutes. Add walnuts, pepper, celery powder and nutmeg. Bring to a boil, reduce heat and simmer, uncovered, 10 minutes. Remove from heat and add cream. Heat through over low heat 5 minutes.

Makes 4 servings.

Main Course

These special soups are meant to be main course dishes. Add a salad, bread and your favorite beverage and you have an entire meal! Some of these recipes are old favorites, and it will be well worth your time to make large quantities for freezing or refrigerating, because the leftovers are usually just as popular.

Paprika Chicken

A spicy recipe to jazz up your chicken soup. The spiciness is mellowed by the coolness of the yogurt. A red or white wine spritzer is very refreshing with this soup.

4	cloves garlic, minced
1	large onion, chopped
4	Tablespoons butter
2¹/₂	cups fresh white mushrooms, sliced
1	fryer (2¹/₂ pounds), cut into 8 pieces
4	cups chicken stock
3	Tablespoons flour
	white pepper
2	Tablespoons Hungarian paprika
1¹/₂	cups plain yogurt
	minced fresh parsley

In a large soup pot sauté garlic and onion in butter for 5 minutes. Add mushrooms and sauté another 5 minutes. Rinse and pat dry chicken pieces. Add chicken and stock to the soup pot. Cover, bring to a boil, reduce heat and simmer 45 minutes.

Remove chicken pieces with a slotted spoon. Allow to cool enough to separate meat from skin and bones. Discard skin and bones, dice meat and return to soup. Whisk in flour and stir occasionally until thickened, about 10 minutes. Add white pepper to taste. Stir in paprika and yogurt and heat through. Sprinkle minced fresh parsley over each portion.

Makes 6 to 8 servings.

Old-Fashioned Bean With Ham

Start this soup in the morning and let it simmer all day. You'll be rewarded with a richer-tasting soup and a heady aroma filling your house. A tall, cold glass of milk is the perfect mate.

1 *pound dried Great Northern beans, rinsed,*
  drained and picked over
2 *smoked ham hocks (about 2 pounds)*
1 *large onion, chopped*
4 *cloves garlic, minced*
1 *bay leaf*
1 *medium potato, pared and cubed*
2 *ribs celery, finely chopped*
1 *large carrot, shredded*
2 *Tablespoons fresh parsley, minced cracked black pepper*

In a large soup pot combine beans and 2½ quarts of water. Discard any beans that float to the surface. Bring to a boil, cover, continue to boil 2 minutes. Remove from heat and allow pot to stand, covered, 1 hour.

Add ham hocks, onion, garlic and bay leaf. Cover, bring to a boil, reduce heat and simmer 2 hours. Add potatoes, celery, carrot and parsley. Cover and continue simmering, at least 1 hour or longer (all day if you wish).

Remove ham hocks and bay leaf with a slotted spoon. Separate meat from fat and bones, dice meat and return to the soup. Discard fat and bones. Season to taste with black pepper.

Do not freeze.

Makes 6 hearty servings and this recipe is easily doubled.

Traditional Brunswick Stew

The recipe for this stew had its beginnings in North Carolina. Originally this dish called for rabbit, possum or whatever was available at stew time. I've modified this recipe, using pork and chicken, to make it easier for folks who do their game hunting in grocery stores. Start preparing this stew 24 hours in advance.

$2^1/2$ pounds pork roast
1   Tablespoon cayenne pepper or chili pepper
1   5 to 6 pound fryer, cut up into 8 pieces
3   cans (18 ounces each) whole, peeled tomatoes
1   large yellow onion, chopped
2   cans (15 ounces each) butter beans, drained
2   cans (15 ounces each) cream-style corn
$^3/4$ cup Worcestershire sauce
4   cups mashed potatoes (instant may be used)
$^1/3$ cup butter
2   teaspoons hot pepper or Tabasco sauce

First Day: Place pork roast in a large stew or stock pot and add enough water to cover. Add $1^1/2$ teaspoons of the cayenne or chili pepper. Cover, bring to a boil, reduce heat to very low and simmer $2^1/2$ hours. Add chicken pieces (skins may be removed for less fat in the stew) and remaining chili pepper. Reheat to boiling, reduce heat and simmer $1^1/2$ hours or until meat starts to fall from the bone. Remove the chicken and pork and set aside to cool. Reserve the stock.

When meat is cool enough to handle, use your fingers to separate the chicken from the skin and bones. Shred all of the meat into a large bowl. Add 3 cups of the stock to the meat, cover and refrigerate overnight. (The remaining stock can be degreased and frozen for future use.)

Next Day: Return meat/stock mixture to the pot. Drain and roughly chop the tomatoes and add to the meat along with the onion. Simmer, covered, 2 hours. Add remaining ingredients, blend well and simmer 1 to 2 hours longer.

Make sure that your dining table is bright and cheery enough to balance the stew's lackluster appearance.

Makes 15 servings.

Split Pea Soup

A velvety appetizer when served with a sprinkle of croutons and a very dry sherry. It becomes a main course dish with the addition of a smoked Polish sausage, sliced on the diagonal and added about $1/2$ hour before serving.

1   *pound dried split green peas, rinsed, drained and picked over*
2   *large ham hocks (about 2 pounds)*
9   *cups water*
4   *strips bacon or salt pork, chopped*
2   *medium onions, chopped*
2   *ribs celery, chopped*
1   *bay leaf*
     pinch of rosemary
$1/4$ *cup fresh parsley, minced dry sherry*
     Croutons*

In a large stock or soup pot, place peas and ham hocks in the water. Bring to a boil, reduce heat and simmer, covered, 45 minutes. Sauté pork or bacon in a skillet until crisp. Add onions and celery and continue to sauté 8 to 10 minutes. Add the sauté mixture to the peas along with the bay leaf, rosemary and parsley. Cover and simmer 2 hours. Remove ham hocks with a slotted spoon and set aside to cool.

When cooled, separate meat from fat and bones. Discard fat and bones, dice meat and return to the soup. (This step is optional if you prefer your soup meatless.) Simmer soup 30 minutes, covered, just before serving. Remove bay leaf.

Serve a small glass of dry sherry with the soup. The sherry may be poured into the soup or sipped alongside it. Sprinkle a handful of croutons on each portion.

Makes 8 appetizer servings or 6 main course bowls.

*Croutons: 2 slices of sourdough bread, (crusts trimmed), 2 tablespoons butter and one dash each of garlic powder, onion powder, paprika and ground black pepper. Slice bread into $1/4$-inch strips and then crosswise into $1/4$-inch cubes. Sauté cubes in butter and spices until golden brown.

Makes about 2 cups.

Irish Beef Stew

Serve with the same beer that you use in the recipe. Irish soda bread, topped with sweet butter, is wonderful for soaking up the rich gravy.

2 pounds stewing beef, chuck or round cuts
1/3 cup cooking oil
1 bottle (12 ounces) dark Irish beer or ale
1 pound baby carrots, fresh or frozen
1 pound pearl onions, fresh or frozen
5 cups new potatoes, pared and left whole
2 cups rich or reduced beef stock
4 cloves garlic, minced
1 Tablespoon fresh parsley, minced ground black pepper
1 Tablespoon cornstarch
1/3 cup water

Cut beef into bite-size chunks. Do not trim fat because it keeps the meat tender during the cooking process. In a large Dutch oven heat oil over medium heat. Lightly brown beef, in two batches if necessary. Return all beef to the pot.

Add the beer or ale, vegetables and stock. Cover and simmer 30 to 45 minutes.

Add garlic, parsley and pepper to taste. Cover and continue to simmer over medium heat 1 hour. Combine cornstarch with 1/3 cup water and blend well. Stir into stew and simmer, uncovered, 30 minutes. At this point the stew may be served, but longer cooking only improves the flavor.

Refrigerates for 3 days. Do not freeze as the consistency will change, presenting an unsavory appearance.

Makes 8 servings.

Polish Pork Stew

A change of pace from the usual beef stews, this pork stew is a real treat on a cold winter evening. Your favorite dark beer or ale goes perfectly with this savory dish.

1   *pound boneless pork shoulder*
2   *Tablespoons cooking oil*
2   *Tablespoons flour*
1   *large onion, chopped*
1   *rib celery, chopped*
4   *cups beef stock*
1   *Tablespoon parsley, minced*
½   *cup pearl barley*
1   *teaspoon caraway seeds*
¼   *teaspoon rosemary*
    cracked black pepper
4   *cups green cabbage, thinly sliced*
½   *pound fresh white mushrooms, sliced*
1   *Polish sausage (Kielbasa), sliced diagonally*

Cut pork shoulder into 1-inch cubes. Do not trim fat because it keeps the meat tender during the cooking process. Brown pork in oil in a large Dutch oven. Sprinkle flour over pork. Add onion and celery. Toss to combine and sauté 5 minutes.

Add stock, parsley, barley, caraway seeds, rosemary and pepper to taste. Bring to a boil, cover, reduce heat and simmer 30 minutes. Add cabbage, mushrooms and sausage. Continue to simmer, at least 1 hour longer or all day, if you wish.

Ladle into warmed bowls and garnish with fresh parsley sprigs. **Makes 6 to 8 servings.**

Cook-off Chili

Once you taste this chili, you'll know why it's an award winner. This is a traditional chili and very rich, so you may want to add red kidney beans. It can simmer all day long, because time only improves the flavor. This chili is medium spicy, so keep test-testing as you go along to prevent an over-fiery chili.

$^{1}/_{2}$ cup cooking oil
3 ribs celery, peeled and diced
4 yellow onions, minced
14 cloves garlic, minced
3 Jalapeña peppers, peeled, seeded and diced
12 ounces medium-hot chilis, diced
3 Tablespoons fresh cilantro, minced
3 pounds ground beef
$2^{1}/_{4}$ pounds ground pork
3 cans ($14^{1}/_{2}$ ounces each) whole, peeled tomatoes, seeded and finely chopped
1 Tablespoon ground cumin
$1^{1}/_{2}$ cups plus 4 Tablespoons chili powder
3 bay leaves
6 Tablespoons dark tequila
6 Tablespoons dark imported beer
a few shakes of hot pepper sauce
6 cans (15 ounces each) tomato sauce
6 Tablespoons tomato paste
$1^{1}/_{2}$ teaspoons ground oregano
$^{1}/_{4}$ teaspoon ground cinnamon
$1^{1}/_{2}$ squares ($1^{1}/_{2}$ ounces) semisweet chocolate

Heat oil in a large skillet over low heat. Add the celery, onions, garlic, peppers, chili and cilantro and sauté 15 minutes. In another large skillet, sauté the beef and pork until no pink remains in the meat. Drain meat in paper toweling to absorb grease. When meat has cooled, mince finely with a cleaver. Combine the sautéed vegetables, minced meat and remaining ingredients, in the order they are listed, and add to the chili pot. Stir well and simmer at least 2 hours.

Makes approximately 1½ gallons.

Far Western Soup

A special combination of western flavors make for a hearty meal. Pass around a plate of cornbread, spiked with bacon and onion, and serve with tall glasses of cold milk or beer.

1   fryer (2¹/₂ pounds), cut into 8 pieces
2   quarts water
2   medium onions, quartered
2   bay leaves, crushed
10 black pepper corns
3   Tablespoons brown rice uncooked
2   teaspoons oregano
1   teaspoon dried cilantro
1   can (15¹/₂ ounces) garbanzo beans, undrained
3   Tablespoons mild chills, seeded and diced
2   cups Monterey Jack cheese, grated

In a large soup pot combine rinsed and dried chicken pieces (without skins if you prefer), water, onions, bay leaves and peppercorns. Cover, bring to a boil, reduce heat and simmer 1 hour.

Remove chicken with a slotted spoon and set aside to cool. Strain stock and return to a rinsed-out soup pot. Add rice, oregano and cilantro. Cover, bring to a second boil and simmer 20 minutes. Add beans, their liquid and chilis.

Separate chicken meat from skin and bones. Discard bones, dice meat and add to soup. Sprinkle cheese on top. Heat 10 minutes before serving to allow cheese to melt.

Makes 8 to 10 servings.

Chowders

A true chowder recipe contains no flour or cornstarch. The starch in the potatoes acts as the thickening agent.

As with all chowders, these soups are best left to ripen overnight in the refrigerator and then served the next day.

Use fresh clams and seafood whenever possible. The broth from steaming the clams can be used with the fish stock. Always discard any clams or mussels that don't open during cooking.

Oyster Chowder

To cut through the heavy richness of this soup, serve a chilled Chablis or Chardonnay. Pass around a basket of oyster crackers.

> *2 cups potatoes, pared and diced*
> *1 small onion, chopped*
> *1 cup fish stock*
> *1 cup fresh or canned shucked oysters, undrained and*
> *   roughly chopped*
> *1 cup oyster liquid*
> *1 cup light cream*
> *¹/₃ cup butter*
> *   pinch of paprika, white pepper*

Place potatoes, onion and fish stock in a large soup pot. Cover and cook over medium heat until potatoes are tender, about 30 minutes. Add oysters and 1 cup of their liquid. (Use water or clam juice to make 1 cup if you do not have enough.) Bring to a boil and remove from heat. Stir in cream, butter and spices to taste. Cook over low heat until butter is melted. Overcooking the oysters will make them tough.

Can freeze for up to 1 month.

Makes 6 servings.

Lighten Up: To lower fat and calories, substitute the following for the heavy cream. In a saucepan, combine 1/4 cup nonfat dry milk, 1¹/₂ tablespoons cornstarch and 1 cup water. Stir over low heat until thick, then add to soup in place of cream.

New England Clam Chowder

Probably the most popular type of chowder. A Green Hungarian wine sounds like a strange companion, but it goes well with this wonderful chowder.

3   *cups fish stock*
4   *medium potatoes, pared and diced*
4   *strips bacon or salt pork*
1   *large onion, chopped*
3   *cups chopped clams, fresh or canned*
2   *cloves garlic, minced*
    pinch of thyme
3   *Tablespoons butter*
4¹/₂   *cups light cream*
    white pepper

Place fish stock and potatoes in a medium soup pot and simmer, covered, 1 hour. Sauté bacon or salt pork in a skillet. Remove and drain on paper toweling. When cooled, crumble the bacon or dice the salt pork.

In remaining drippings, sauté onion 3 minutes. Add the crumbled bacon or pork and set aside. When the potatoes are tender, add clams, onion mixture, garlic, thyme and butter. Add light cream and stir gently. Add white pepper to taste.

Do not allow this soup to boil. Ladle into warmed bowls and serve with tiny oyster crackers. Float a pat of butter on top of each portion for added richness.

Keeps 3 days in the refrigerator.

Makes 6 to 8 servings.

Lighten Up: To lower fat and calories, substitute the following for the heavy cream. In a saucepan, combine 1 cup nonfat dry milk, 1/3 cup cornstarch and 4¹/₂ cups water. Stir over low heat until thick, then add to soup in place of cream.

Manhattan Clam Chowder

This is a red tomato soup unlike the creamy white of New England style. Serve with garlic French bread. A hearty red wine like Burgundy or Zinfandel goes well with this chowder.

3	strips bacon or salt pork
1	medium onion, chopped
3	cups Fish stock
3	cups potatoes, pared and diced
2	cups tomatoes, peeled and diced
$^1/_4$	cup tomato juice
$^1/_4$	cup green Bell pepper, seeded and diced
2	cloves garlic, minced
1	bay leaf
3	Tablespoons butter
$2^1/_2$	cups minced clams, fresh or canned
	ground black pepper

Sauté bacon or salt pork in a medium soup pot until crisp. Remove and drain on paper toweling, crumble or dice when cooled. To the remaining drippings, add the chopped onion and sauté for 5 minutes. Add fish stock, potatoes, tomatoes and juice, pepper, garlic and bay leaf. Simmer, covered, until potatoes are tender, about 45 minutes. Stir in crumbled bacon or pork, butter and clams. When butter melts, season with black pepper.

Makes 8 servings.

Lighten Up: To lower fat and calories, substitute the following for the heavy cream. In a saucepan, combine 1/2 cup nonfat dry milk, 3 tablespoons cornstarch and 2 cups water. Stir over low heat until thick, then add to soup in place of cream.

Corn Chowder

A great way to use fresh corn during the summer months, but equally as convenient to make in the off season using frozen or canned corn.

4	bacon strips
1	medium onion, chopped
3	cloves garlic, minced
1	rib celery, chopped
2	cups chicken stock
2	medium baking potatoes, pared and diced
2½	cups corn kernels, fresh*, frozen or canned
2½	cups heavy cream
	pinch of nutmeg
	white pepper

Sauté the bacon in a medium soup pot, turning often to prevent sticking. Remove cooked bacon to paper toweling to absorb the grease; reserve pan drippings. Crumble bacon when cooked and set aside. In the reserved drippings, sauté the onion, garlic and celery until softened. Add stock and potatoes, cover and simmer 30 minutes over medium heat. Add corn and cream, stir well.

Cover and cook over low heat for 15 minutes. Add the bacon, nutmeg and white pepper to taste. Stir gently and allow chowder to rest 15 minutes before serving. As with most chowders, this soup's flavor and consistency is much improved after an overnight stay in the refrigerator and a gentle reheating.

Hint: *To prepare fresh corn from the cob: parboil ears for 3 minutes, then cool slightly. Using a sharp knife, scrape downward to remove kernels.

Makes 5 to 6 servings.

Lighten Up: To lower fat and calories, substitute the following for the heavy cream. In a saucepan, combine 1/2 cup nonfat dry milk, 3 tablespoons cornstarch and 2½ cups water. Stir over low heat until thick, then add to soup in place of cream.

Turkey Chowder

This chowder is the answer to the question, "What do I do with my leftover Thanksgiving turkey carcass?" Again, as with most chowders, it is better if left to ripen overnight in the refrigerator.

3   cups chicken stock
4   medium potatoes, pared and diced
4   strips bacon or salt pork
1   large onion, chopped
3   cups cooked turkey meat*, chopped
4   cloves garlic, minced
    pinch of thyme
3   Tablespoons butter
4¹/₂ cups light cream
    white pepper

*Duck or goose may be substituted.

Place chicken stock and potatoes in a medium soup pot and simmer, covered, 1 hour. Cook bacon or salt pork in a skillet and set aside on paper toweling to drain. Crumble when cooled. Reserve pan drippings.

In reserved drippings, sauté the onion 3 minutes. Combine the crumbled bacon with the onion and set aside.

When the potatoes are tender, add turkey meat, onion mixture, garlic, thyme and butter. When the butter melts, slowly pour in the cream. Season with white pepper. **Do not allow chowder to boil.**

Ladle into warm bowls and float a pat of butter on top. Serve with oyster crackers.

Makes 6 to 8 servings.

Lighten Up: To lower fat and calories, substitute the following for the heavy cream. In a saucepan, combine 1 cup nonfat dry milk, 1/3 cup cornstarch and 4¹/₂ cups water. Stir over low heat until thick, then add to soup in place of cream.

From the Sea

Seafood Bisque

This bisque is an attractive first course soup for an elegant luncheon. It is equally good when served chilled with thin slices of lemon. This seafood bisque deserves a good Sauvignon or Fumé Blanc.

2   *Tablespoons butter*
2   *medium leeks, white parts only, chopped*
1   *medium carrot, pared and diced*
1   *medium onion, chopped*
1/4   *teaspoon thyme*
1   *cup fish stock*
2   *cups heavy cream*
1/2   *cup dry vermouth*
3   *ounces salmon, boneless and cubed*
1/2   *pound bay scallops (reserve 5 or 6)*
1/2   *cup tiny shrimp*
    white pepper
    cayenne pepper
    parsley sprigs or lemon slices

In a 3-quart saucepan melt butter, then sauté leeks, carrot, onion and thyme until softened, about 10 minutes. Add stock, cream, vermouth, salmon and scallops. Cook over very low heat 5 minutes (a few minutes longer, if seafood is frozen). Strain soup through a sieve.

Purée solids in a blender or food processor. Return stock and purée to the saucepan. Stir until blended and add reserved scallops and shrimp. Season to taste with white and cayenne peppers. Heat bisque through but do not boil. Garnish with parsley sprigs or lemon slices if serving chilled.

Variation: Use 3/4 pound of shrimp, scallops or salmon instead of the salmon/scallops combination and follow the above recipe.

Makes 4 servings.

Lighten Up: To lower fat and calories, substitute the following for the heavy cream. In a saucepan, combine 1/2 cup nonfat dry milk, 3 tablespoons cornstarch and 2 cups water. Stir over low heat until thick, then add to soup in place of cream.

Shrimp Gumbo

The southern seafood classic is made with file powder for an authentic taste. Ladle over bowls of fluffy white rice for a main course dish.

2   quarts * chicken stock
2   pounds large shrimp, shelled and deveined
3   Tablespoons butter
1   large onion, chopped
4   cloves garlic, minced
1   rib celery, chopped
1   large green bell pepper, seeded and diced
1/2   cup corn kernels, fresh, frozen or canned
1   cup chopped okra, fresh or canned
2   cups peeled tomatoes, chopped
1/4   cup fresh parsley, minced
2   Tablespoons uncooked white rice
1/2   teaspoon paprika
1   teaspoon filé powder
    ground black pepper

In a medium saucepan, bring 6 cups of stock to boil. Drop raw shrimp into boiling stock and cook 1 minute. Remove shrimp with a slotted spoon and set aside. Strain stock through a cheesecloth-lined sieve into a large soup pot.

In a skillet melt butter and sauté onion, garlic, celery and Bell pepper for 10 minutes. Add sautéed vegetables to stock along with remaining vegetables, rice and paprika. Add 2 cups of the remaining stock.

Mix filé powder with a little water and add to soup. Cover, bring to a boil, reduce heat and simmer 30 minutes. Add shrimp 5 minutes before serving.

Do not overcook gumbo or the filé will become stringy and ruin the soup.

*Hint: More or less of the stock may be used depending on the preferred thickness.

Makes 8 servings.

San Francisco Crab Pot

San Francisco is famous for its history, tourist attractions, wharves, restaurants and seafood. This soup most reminds me of the sights, sounds and smells of the City by the Bay, and it is hearty enough to be a main course meal. Serve with San Francisco sourdough bread, a Caesar salad and a good California Cabernet Sauvignon.

4	cups chicken stock
4	cups beef stock
2	cups water
1	large onion, chopped
2	large carrots, pared and diced
2	medium potatoes, pared and diced
2	ribs celery, chopped
3	medium zucchini (Italian squash), diced
1	cup corn kernels, fresh, frozen or canned
$1/4$	cup pearl barley
$1/4$	cup dried split peas, yellow or green variety
1	package (9 ounces) frozen sweet peas
1	package (9 ounces) frozen baby lima beans
2	cups smoked ham, diced
1	can (28 ounces) peeled tomatoes, undrained and chopped
1	bay leaf
$1/2$	teaspoon each basil and thyme
$1/4$	teaspoon rosemary
	ground black pepper
12-16	ounces fresh or frozen crab meat

Combine all of the above ingredients except for the crab in a large stock pot. Cover, bring to a boil, reduce heat and simmer $1\frac{1}{2}$ to 2 hours.

Just before serving, add the crab meat. Stir until warmed through and serve immediately. This soup can be cooked all day if you wish as long as the crab is added only at the last minute.

Keeps 4 days in the refrigerator.

Makes 10 to 12 servings.

Cioppino

This fish stew is Italian in origin, though no one seems to know exactly how the name translates. The word "cioppino" is not found in the Italian language. No matter, the taste of cioppino is unique. It is definitely for special occasions—serve in a fancy tureen that doubles as a centerpiece. Serve hot garlic bread and a salad dressed with an olive oil vinaigrette. Accompany with your favorite dry Italian red wine.

$1/3$ cup virgin olive oil
3   large onions, chopped
4   cloves garlic, minced
2   cups dry red wine
$1/2$ cup parsley, finely chopped
$1^1/2$ teaspoons each basil and oregano
$1/4$ teaspoon cayenne pepper
1   can (12 ounces) tomato sauce
1   can (28 ounces) peeled tomatoes, drained and chopped
1   pound large, raw shrimp, shelled and deveined
3   pounds fillets of sea bass, halibut or cod
1   pound scallops
2   dozen clams or mussels in shell
2   pounds cracked crab in shell (lobster tails in shell may be used)

Heat oil in a large soup pot and sauté onions 10 minutes. Add garlic, wine, parsley, basil, oregano and cayenne pepper. Simmer 10 minutes over medium heat. Add tomatoes and sauce, and continue simmering over low heat 30 minutes.

Cut shrimp, fish and scallops into bite-size pieces, add to soup and simmer 30 minutes. If using pre-cooked shrimp or crab, add to soup 10 minutes before serving to prevent overcooking. Steam clams and mussels separately. Discard any that do not open. Set aside, and add just before serving. Ladle into warmed bowls, leaving the clams or mussels in their shells. **Makes 10 servings.**

International

This collection of international recipes is a small sampling of the many that I've gathered in my travels. They are my favorites. Each one is especially indicative of its country's cuisine. I know that you'll enjoy them as much as I do.

Avgolemono

The national chicken-lemon soup of the Greek Islands is surprisingly fast and easy to make. Serve it with one of Greece's fine dry white wines.

4   *cups chicken stock*
¼   *cup uncooked white rice*
     dash of nutmeg
3   *egg yolks*
     juice of 1 large lemon
     parsley sprigs

In a medium saucepan combine stock, rice and nutmeg. Simmer 30 minutes or until rice is tender.

Lightly beat egg yolks and lemon juice together. Stir a spoonful of the hot soup in with the egg mixture. Add the egg mixture to the soup. Stir constantly 3 minutes. **Do not allow soup to boil.**

Garnish with sprigs of fresh parsley.

Do not freeze. The eggs will cause separation and curdling when reheated.

Makes 4 first course servings.

African Peanut Soup

A main course soup that's colorful and filling.

3   Tablespoons peanut oil
1   medium onion, chopped
1   large carrot, pared and diced
1   rib celery, chopped
1   green or red Bell pepper, seeded and sliced
3   Tablespoons flour
5   cups chicken stock
$^{1}/_{2}$ cup creamy or chunk-style peanut butter
2   large tomatoes, peeled, seeded and diced
2   cups cooked chicken meat, diced
1   cup milk
    white pepper
    cayenne pepper
    chopped roasted peanuts

Heat oil in a 3-quart saucepan. Sauté onion, carrot, celery and pepper 10 minutes. Stir in flour and slowly whisk in chicken stock. Stirring frequently, heat to boiling.

Add peanut butter and simmer 15 minutes. Add tomatoes, chicken meat and milk. Season to taste with white and cayenne pepper and simmer 30 additional minutes before serving.

Garnish with a handful of chopped roasted peanuts on each portion.

Makes 6 servings.

Guatemalan Black Bean Soup

My all-time favorite from Guatemala. By adding the traditional condiments of cooked white rice and minced white onions, you will have the true flavor of this Guatemalan specialty.

This soup makes a dramatic starter for a Latin-style dinner. The black color of the beans is unusual for soup, so colorful foods should be served for contrast.

1	pound dried black beans, rinsed, drained and picked over
1¹/₂	cups celery, chopped
2	medium white onions, chopped
¹/₂	teaspoon black pepper
1	bay leaf
2	smoked ham hocks (about 2 pounds)
¹/₂	cup dry sherry
	cooked white rice
	minced white onion

In a large soup pot combine beans and 2 quarts of water. Discard any beans that float to the surface. Bring to a boil, cover and boil 2 minutes. Remove from heat and allow to stand 1 hour, covered.

Add celery, onion, pepper, bay leaf and ham hocks. Bring to a boil, reduce heat and simmer, covered, 2 hours. Discard bay leaf and remove ham hocks with a slotted spoon. Strain soup through a sieve. Return stock to pot.

In a food processor or blender, purée beans, in 2 batches if necessary. Return to pot. Separate ham meat from fat and bones. Discard fat and bones, dice meat and add to pot. Add sherry and heat soup through until gently simmering. Water may be added to thin the soup if it becomes too thick.

Garnish with cooked white rice and minced white onions to taste.

Makes 4 to 6 servings.

Minestrone

A vegetable lover's delight! Serve with peasant bread drizzled with olive oil, salad and a dry red wine. Spumoni makes the perfect cooling dessert.

1½ quarts chicken stock or water
1 medium white onion, chopped
3 cloves garlic, minced
1 leek, well-rinsed and sliced
2 Tablespoons fresh parsley, minced
3 Tablespoons tomato paste
3 ribs celery, chopped
2 large carrots, pared and sliced
2 cups green or purple cabbage, shredded
2 medium zucchini (Italian squash)
1 can (28 ounces) tomatoes, chopped
¼ teaspoon each: thyme, oregano, basil, sage, rosemary and marjoram
½ teaspoon ground black pepper
1 can (28 ounces) red kidney beans
⅓ cup uncooked brown rice

Place all ingredients in a large soup pot except for the beans and rice. Bring to a boil, add the rice and simmer, covered, 1 hour. Rinse and drain beans to remove canning solution. Add beans to pot.

This soup can be cooked on very low heat for up to 7 hours for added richness.

Makes 6 to 8 servings.

Mulligatawny

A spicy, golden soup from India. I've tasted this soup in restaurants all over the world, and still think this recipe is the best.

12   cloves garlic, minced
2   1-inch pieces fresh ginger peeled and chopped
1   teaspoon each: ground cumin, cayenne pepper, ground
       coriander and black pepper
1/2 teaspoon each turmeric and curry powder
2   Tablespoons water
4   Tablespoons vegetable oil
1   pound lean ground beef
1   large onion, chopped
2   quarts chicken stock
4   Tablespoons uncooked brown rice
6   Tablespoons cornstarch
1/2 cup water
2   Tablespoons each lemon and lime juice
       coriander or mint sprigs for garnish
       fried onion rings for garnish

Combine the garlic, ginger, cumin, cayenne, coriander, black pepper, turmeric and curry powder with 2 tablespoons of water and mash into a coarse paste. In a large pot heat oil over medium heat. Add ground beef, onion and spice paste and cook 15 minutes or until all of the meat is well browned. Add stock and rice and bring to a boil.

In a small cup blend cornstarch and water until smooth. Add to soup and stir constantly to reheat to boiling. Cover, reduce heat and simmer 40 minutes.

Add lemon and lime juices. Stir well and serve hot in small bowls for an appetizer or over bowls of white rice for a main course dish. Garnish with coriander or mint sprigs and crispy, fried onion rings.

Makes 10 servings.

Bourride-Garlic Fish Soup

1   large onion, chopped
1   large carrot, pared and sliced
1   leek, well-rinsed and sliced
4   cloves garlic, minced
3   Tablespoons cooking oil
2   cups water
2   cups dry white wine
1   teaspoon each orange peel, thyme and fennel seeds
1   bay leaf
    white pepper
    Garlic Mayonnaise-recipe follows
4   egg yolks
4   pounds fresh salt water fish in any combination
    (sea bass, sole, cod, flounder and halibut)

In a medium soup pot, sauté onion, carrot, leek and garlic in oil for 10 minutes. Add water, wine, spices and simmer, uncovered, 30 minutes. In the meantime, prepare the Garlic Mayonnaise.

Strain the stock through a cheesecloth-lined sieve. Return the strained stock to the pot and bring to a boil. Add the fish, which has been cut into bite-size pieces, to the boiling stock in three batches. Cook each batch 2 minutes. Remove fish from stock and set aside in a warm oven and keep tightly covered so fish won't dry out.

Combine the yolks with 1 cup of the mayonnaise. Spoon a little of the hot stock into the egg mixture, blend and return to the soup. Stir gently over very low heat until the soup starts to thicken. **Do not allow soup to boil at this point** or it will curdle.

Place the warmed reserved fish in the bottoms of the deep bowls and ladle the soup over the fish.

Serve with lots of crusty, hot french bread and sweet butter. For a complete meal, add a Salade Niçoise and a white French Burgundy.

Makes 8 main course servings.

Garlic Mayonnaise: Makes 1 cup

1   *egg yolk*
5   *cloves garlic, minced*
³/₄ *cup virgin olive oil*
2   *teaspoons lemon juice*
     white pepper

Whisk egg yolk and garlic together in a small deep bowl. Continuing to whisk, slowly pour in oil until sauce begins to thicken. Whisk 3 minutes longer. Add lemon juice and white pepper to taste. Refrigerate, covered, until ready to use.

Soup À L'oignon, Gratinée

6   *medium white onions, thinly sliced*
8   *cloves garlic, minced*
¹/₂ *cup butter*
2   *quarts beef broth*
1   *cup dry sherry or Cognac generous pinch of dried marjoram black pepper*
     french bread
     Gruyère or Port Salut cheese

In a medium soup pot, sauté onion and garlic in butter for 15 minutes. Add broth, sherry or Cognac and marjoram. Cover, bring to a boil, reduce heat and simmer 1 hour. Add black pepper to taste during the simmer.

Before serving, pre-heat oven to broil. Ladle soup into ovenproof bowls. Spoon in 1 tablespoon of sherry or Cognac but do not stir. Top soup with a slice of french bread covered with a generous amount of Gruyère or Port Salut cheese. Place bowls at least 6 inches from the broiler and heat until the cheese bubbles.

By adding a substantial salad such as spinach or seafood, partnered with a dry white wine, you have the makings of a light and marvelous dinner.

Makes 6 hearty servings or 8 smaller appetizer portions.

Soupe Au Pistou Basil Vegetable

A vegetable soup flavored with a fresh basil sauce. For premium results, the ingredients, especially the basil, should be fresh.

Peasant bread or rolls, a tossed salad and fresh fruit for dessert complete this meal. A mature Côtes du Rhone is an ideal wine.

1	pound dried Great Northern beans, rinsed, drained and picked over
$1/2$	pound lima beans
1	Tablespoon olive oil
$1/2$	cup lean salt pork, chopped
4	large onions, chopped
6	ribs celery, chopped
4	large carrots, pared and sliced
1	leek, well-rinsed and sliced
$1/2$	pound green beans, trimmed and roughly chopped
6	potatoes, pared and cubed
1	large turnip, pared and cubed
5	large zucchini (Italian squash), chopped
$1/2$	head green cabbage, shredded
2	bay leaves
$1/4$	teaspoon sage
	ground black pepper
2	quarts water
	grated swiss cheese Pistou—recipe follows

In a large saucepan combine beans and enough water to cover. Discard any beans that float to the surface. Boil the beans for $1/2$ hour. Drain and set aside. If the lima beans are fresh, shell and blanch them.

Heat oil in the bottom of a large soup or stock pot. Sauté salt pork and onions 5 minutes. Add celery, carrots and leek and saute another 5 minutes. Add the remaining ingredients, including the beans, to the pot and cover with water. Cover, bring to a boil, reduce heat and simmer 45 minutes to 1 hour or until vegetables are tender. While the soup is simmering, prepare the Pistou.

Makes 6 servings.

Pistou

2¹/₂-3 *cups fresh basil leaves, well-rinsed*
4-6 *cloves garlic, minced*
1 *teaspoon fresh parsley minced*
¹/₂ *cup grated swiss cheese (or semi-hard cheese)*
¹/₂ *cup virgin olive oil*

Roughly chop basil. Combine basil, garlic and parsley in a food processor, blender, or use a mortar and pestle to form a smooth paste. Blend in cheese. In a thin stream, slowly pour in the oil until blended. Refrigerate, covered, until just before serving the soup.

Add all of the sauce if you are serving the entire pot of soup. If you wish to refrigerate or freeze any of the soup, add 2 tablespoons of the Pistou to each portion that you are serving and stir well. The soup and Pistou will separate if they are frozen together. Pass around the grated swiss cheese as a topping.

Caldo Verde

The Portuguese national soup. A dry red Portuguese or Spanish wine best accompanies this dish.

¹/₄ *cup virgin olive oil*
2 *medium onions, chopped*
4 *cloves garlic, minced*
3 *medium potatoes, pared and diced*
2 *quarts chicken stock*
3 *cups green cabbage, thinly sliced*
3 *cups fresh spinach, well-rinsed, stemmed and thinly sliced*
¹/₂ *teaspoon white pepper*

In a large pot, heat oil and sauté onions and garlic 10 minutes. Add potatoes and sauté an additional 10 minutes. Add stock, cover and simmer 2 hours. Add cabbage, spinach and pepper. Simmer, uncovered, 45 minutes or longer.

Variation: For a cream version of Caldo Verde, follow the above recipe until the cabbage and spinach have simmered 45 minutes. Remove soup from heat and separate solids from stock with a sieve. Return stock to pot. Purée solids in a food processor or blender. Return to soup and add 1/2 cup light cream. Stir gently to combine. **Heat soup until hot but not boiling.**

Makes 6 to 8 servings.

Borscht

It is said that there are as many ways to make Borscht as there are Russians. The only common ingredients that appeared in all of the recipes that I read or tested were beets and sour cream, both of which are in this version. Be careful when peeling and grating the beets because the juice will stain.

Borscht can be served hot or cold.

    2   large ham hocks (about 2 pounds)
    4   cups beef stock
    8   medium beets
    1   carrot, pared and shredded
    ¹/₂ head red cabbage, shredded
    1   medium onion, shredded
    1   Tablespoon butter
    1   Tablespoon white vinegar ground black pepper
        sour cream

Place ham hocks and beef stock in a large soup or stock pot. Bring to a boil, reduce heat and simmer, covered, 2 hours. Peel and grate beets. Combine beets with carrot, cabbage and onion. Remove ham hocks from the stock and set aside to cool. Add beet mixture to stock and simmer, covered, 20 minutes.

Separate ham meat from fat and bones. Discard fat and bones, dice meat and return to soup along with butter, vinegar and pepper. Extra beef stock may be added if the soup is too thick. Simmer an additional 20 minutes.

Spoon a dollop of sour cream on each portion.

Can freeze up to 1 month.

Makes 6 servings.

Cold Soups

Most Americans equate the word "soup" with a hot, steaming mug on a cold day. So, why not a chilled bowl on a hot day?

Cold soups seem to be widely ignored here in the States. The challenge with cold soup is to make all of the flavors stand out so that taste is your first impression, not temperature. Also, plenty of body is a must for eye and appetite appeal.

Cream of Carrot

A soup to add spice and color to your table.

    3   carrots, scrubbed and sliced
    1   rib celery with leaves, chopped
    1   medium onion, sliced
 1$^1/_2$ cup chicken stock
        dash of cayenne pepper
  $^3/_4$ cup light cream

Place carrots, celery, onion and $^1/_2$ cup of stock in a medium saucepan. Bring to a boil, reduce heat and simmer, covered, 15 minutes.

Pour mixture into a blender and add cayenne pepper. Continue to blend while adding remaining stock and cream. Refrigerate until well chilled.

Due to this soup's richness, serve only in small portions. A sprig of parsley or carrot top is the finishing touch. This soup is perfect as a first course for a lamb dinner. A hearty red Burgundy offsets the spiciness.

Makes 4 to 6 servings.

Cream of Avocado

An extremely rich and creamy soup, California style!

2   large or 3 medium fully ripe avocados
1   cup light cream
2   teaspoons lemon juice
2   cups chicken stock
$^1/_4$ cup dry sherry sour cream lemon wedges

Cut the avocados in half and remove the pits. Scoop out the meat. Place meat, light cream and lemon juice in a food processor or blender and blend to smooth purée. Pour purée into a large bowl and set aside. Heat chicken stock to boiling, skimming foam. Slowly add hot stock to purée and stir in sherry. Refrigerate until well chilled.

Serve in very small portions because this soup is rich. Garnish with a dollop of sour cream and a wedge of lemon. This soup is an excellent first course to a seafood lunch or dinner. Only your best dry white wine is good enough for this soup.

Makes 4 to 6 servings.

Gazpacho

A well-known traditional spicy soup from Spain. Fresh cilantro gives this dish its authentic taste.

6   medium-size fully ripe tomatoes
1   cucumber, peeled and chopped
4   medium-hot chilis, seeded and chopped
3   cloves garlic, minced
1   medium onion, chopped
1/4   cup virgin olive oil
2   Tablespoons red wine vinegar
1   Tablespoon dry sherry
1   Tablespoon fresh cilantro, minced
1/2   cup tomato juice
1/4   cup crushed ice
    Tabasco sauce
    cracked black pepper
    minced fresh parsley
    chopped white onion

Halve and seed tomatoes in a strainer over a large bowl. Press pulp into strainer firmly to extract all juice. Discard pulp and seeds. Chop tomato halves and add to juice. Add remaining vegetables, olive oil, vinegar, sherry and cilantro. Mix well.

Whirl tomato mixture 2 cups at a time in a blender until finely chopped but not liquefied. Return gazpacho to the large bowl and add tomato juice and ice. Use less juice if soup is too liquid. Add a dash of Tabasco sauce and black pepper to taste.

Refrigerate several hours before serving. Sprinkle minced parsley and chopped white onion on top of each portion and serve in ceramic bowls with a basket of tortilla chips.

Variation: I cup of minced clams may be added before refrigerating.

Makes 6 servings.

Cold Cucumber Dill

A fabulous summer luncheon soup. Everyone will beg for your recipe!

  2 *large cucumbers*
  1 *large white onion, chopped*
  3 *cups chicken stock dill weed, fresh or dried white pepper*
  3 *Tablespoons butter*
  3 *Tablespoons flour*
  1 *cup sour cream or plain yogurt*
  1 *cup whipping cream (do not substitute) fresh dill sprigs
      very thin lemon slices*

Peel, seed and chop cucumbers. Place cucumbers, onion and 1½ cups of stock in a heavy covered saucepan. Heat on high until mixture comes to a boil. Reduce heat to medium and simmer, covered, 30 minutes or until cucumbers are soft. Purée in a food processor or blender.

Add a generous pinch of dill weed and white pepper to taste. Melt butter over low heat in a saucepan. Whisk in all of flour and slowly whisk in remaining stock. Cook until slightly thickened. Add cucumber purée and blend in sour cream or yogurt.

In a separate bowl, whip the cream with chilled beaters until soft peaks form. Fold whipped cream into soup very gently. Chill at least 1 hour before serving.

Serve in chilled bowls and garnish with fresh dill sprigs and very thin lemon slices.

Serve with iced tea to cut through the rich creaminess of the soup.

Do not freeze—the soup will lose the body and fluffiness that the whipped cream provides.

Makes 6 appetizer-size servings.

Vichysoisse

There are many versions of this most famous of cold soups. My recipe is very easy to make and its elegance is impressive. (Guests will think you spent hours in the kitchen!) If you wish to serve it hot, it becomes Potato-Leek soup.

6   *leeks, white parts only, well-rinsed and chopped*
1   *large onion, chopped*
3   *Tablespoons butter*
5   *cups chicken stock*
5   *medium potatoes, pared and thinly sliced*
2   *cups heavy cream*
    white pepper
    chopped fresh chives

Saute leeks and onion in butter until soft but not brown in a large, covered soup kettle. Add chicken stock and potatoes. Cover, bring to a boil, reduce heat and simmer 20 minutes or until potatoes are tender. Separate liquid from solids with a strainer.

Process potato mixture in a food processor or blender until they looked whipped. Combine cooking liquid and potato purée in a large bowl. Slowly stir in cream until blended and add white pepper to taste. Refrigerate until well chilled.

Serve in frosted bowls set in ice. Garnish with fresh chopped chives and offer garlic toast on the side. Your driest, most subtle white wine is a perfect complement to this classic soup.

Hint: Vichysoisse can be frozen for up to 2 months but it must be watched carefully during thawing and reheating to avoid any separation. If separation does occur, whirl soup in a blender for 30 seconds to restore to its original consistency.

Makes 8 servings.

Lighten Up: To lower fat and calories, substitute the following for the heavy cream. In a saucepan, combine 1/2 cup nonfat dry milk, 3 tablespoons cornstarch and 2 cups water. Stir over low heat until thick, then add to soup in place of cream.

Dessert

In Europe, cold fruit soups are customarily served as a first course. However, in the United States we tend to think along the lines that sweet foods must be served as dessert. Bring out your favorite dessert wines, ports and sherries to savor with these delicious and different fruit combinations.

Cold Kiwi Soup

I picked up this recipe in New Zealand where Kiwi fruit is king. Its bright green color will surprise and delight your guests.

    2   cups water
    1/2 cup sugar
    4   whole cloves
    1   Tablespoon arrowroot or cornstarch
    2   Tablespoons cold water
    2   pounds Kiwi fruit, fully ripe peel and juice of
         1 large lemon plain yogurt

In a medium saucepan, combine water and sugar and stir until dissolved. Add cloves. Bring to a boil for 5 minutes. Remove cloves.

Combine arrowroot or cornstarch and water to form a paste. Stir paste into the syrup until syrup thickens. Remove from heat.

Reserve 1 peeled and diced Kiwi fruit for garnish. Peel and purée remaining Kiwi fruit. Purée very quickly and lightly or the seeds will be crushed and cause bitterness in the soup. Push puree through a fine sieve or cheesecloth to trap seeds. Add purée to cooled syrup. Refrigerate for several hours until well chilled.

Add grated lemon peel and juice just before serving. Garnish with diced Kiwi fruit and a dollop of yogurt.

Makes 4 servings.

Cold Plum Soup

This soup is made in an instant and can also be used as an unusual topping for ice cream or plain cake. Be sure to use 80 proof rum instead of 151 proof or you'll be serving cold plum cocktails!

1   *can (16 ounces) purple pitted plums, reserve liquid*
¹/₄ *cup lemon or lime juice*
¹/₃ *cup rum (80 proof), light or dark*
    dash of cinnamon

Combine all ingredients in a blender. Process quickly. Refrigerate until chilled. Garnish with mint leaves and a dollop of whipped cream.

Makes 4 servings.

Fruit Soup With Champagne

This soup becomes an elegant dessert with the addition of champagne. Use a good, inexpensive champagne to pour into the soup and sip your best medium-dry champagne along with it.

2   *ripe peaches, pared and sliced (canned may be used)*
1   *can (I 6 ounces) Bing cherries, reserve liquid*
1   *can (I 6 ounces) tart or pie cherries, reserve liquid*
1   *teaspoon each orange peel and cinnamon*
3   *Tablespoons sugar*
2   *Tablespoons cornstarch*
¹/₃ *cup Cointreau or similar orange liqueur*
2   *naval oranges, peeled and sectioned*
1   *bottle (750ml) inexpensive dry champagne*

Combine peaches, cherries and their juice in a large saucepan. Add spices, sugar and cornstarch and stir well. Heat over low heat until mixture boils and thickens. Remove from heat and pour into a large bowl. Add Cointreau and oranges. Stir well and refrigerate until well chilled.

Serve in chilled glass bowls for best effect. Add at least 3 ounces of champagne to each portion just before serving.

Makes 8 servings.

Russian Apple Soup

Living in the United States, we are fortunate to have apples available to us all year long. This Russian recipe struck me as a delightfully different way to use tart apples.

>   3   *medium or 4 small tart apples (Granny Smith, Pippin, etc.)*
> 1¹/₂   *cups water*
>   ¹/₂   *cup sugar cookie crumbs*
>   1   *Tablespoon dry white wine*
>   1   *teaspoon lemon peel*
>   ¹/₂   *cinnamon stick (I -inch)*
> I¹/₂   *cups dry red wine*
>   ¹/₄   *cup sugar*
>   4   *teaspoons lemon juice*
>   1   *Tablespoon any flavor seedless fruit preserves*
>   *sour cream*

Pare, core and quarter apples. Combine apples, water, crumbs, white wine, lemon peel and cinnamon in a large covered saucepan. Cook over medium heat until apples are soft, about 20 minutes.

Strain and press apple mixture through a fine sieve with a wooden spoon. Return apple puree to saucepan. Add red wine, sugar, lemon juice and preserves. Heat over medium heat, stirring constantly until sugar dissolves. Add more sugar or preserves if necessary for sweetening. Refrigerate overnight or until well chilled, about 5 hours. Garnish with a spoonful of sour cream.

Makes 4 servings.